NUMBER AND PLACE VALUES

CRACK THE CODE !!!

🔍 help the detective solve the puzzle

1) *Use the numbers below to create 3 different 4 digit numbers*

RULES

💡 No digit should be repeated

💡 Must use all 4 digits

a) 3 , 4 , 6 , 7

____

____

____

b) 6 , 7 , 8 , 9

____

____

____

c) 2 , 4 , 6 , 9

____

____

____

d) 7 , 3 , 2 , 9

____

____

____

e) 1 , 0 , 1 , 7

____

____

____

f) 0 , 2 , 9 , 6

____

____

____

➤ The hungry Crocodiles Fest !!!

2) *Tot the crocodile is very hungry ! He loves to feat on big numbers……. help him decide*
which number should he eat .

a) 456 _______ 476

b) 532_________ 982

c) 7980 _______3240

d) 164 _______ 123

e) 183 _______0990

f) 494 _______ 7651

🏅 Number race - WHO WINS THE RACE ?

3) *A group of athletes is running a race, but they're not in the correct order. They should be arranged from the smallest to the largest. Can you help them find their proper sequence?*

a) 345 , 678 , 9204

b) 930 , 123 , 12

c) 137 , 190 , 13457

① _______________

② _______________

③ _______________

① _______________

② _______________

③ _______________

① _______________

② _______________

③ _______________

👓 Decode their value?

4) A group of sneaky numbers has hidden their real values! Your mission is to uncover what each digit really stands for

a) 7,679 find the value of 6

b) 8,752 find the value of 2

c) 5,920 find the value of 5

____

____

____

d) 5,687 find the value of 8

e) 347 find the value of 3

f) 8,960 find the value of 0

____

____

____

🪄 Break the spell !!!

*5) Howl the wizard 🧙 ♂ has cast a spell, breaking numbers into parts! Can you **put them back together** to find the real number?*

a) 4000+200+30+2 =

b) 3000+200 +3 =

c) 9000+700+70+1 =

____

____

____

d) 200+40+2 =

e) 8000+60 =

f) 1000+700+90+6 =

____

____

____

🪐Space Explorer's Number Mission!

*Welcome, young **astronauts**! 🧑‍🚀 🧑‍🚀 You are on a mission to **decode secret space coordinates** and unlock the path to new planets. Solve these number riddles to navigate through the galaxy! ☄️*

a)

- ☄ I have **3 digits**.
- ⬍ My **hundreds place** is **4**.
- ⬍ My **tens place** is **half of 4**.
- ⬍ My **one's place** is **double my tens place**.
- 🚀 **What is my secret space code?** Number: _______

b)

- ☄ I have **4 digits**.
- ⬍ My **thousands place** is **7**.
- ⬍ My **hundreds place** is **2 more than my tens place**.
- ⬍ My **one's place** is the **same as my tens place**.
- 🚀 **What is my secret space code?** Number: _______

c)

- ☄ I have **3 digits**.
- ⬍ My **hundreds place** is **5 more than 2**.
- ⬍ My **tens place** is **3 less than my hundreds place**.
- ⬍ My **one's place** is **2 more than my tens place**.
- 🚀 **What is my secret space code?** Number: _______

d)

- ☄ I have **4 digits**.
- ⬍ My **thousands place** is **9**.
- ⬍ My **hundreds place** is **half of my thousands place**.
- ⬍ My **tens place** is **the sum of my hundreds and one's places**.
- ⬍ My **one's place** is **1**.
- 🚀 **What is my secret space code?** Number: _______

e)
✦ I have **3 digits**.

◆ My **hundreds place** is **the sum of 2 and 3**.

◆ My **tens place** is **double my one's place**.

◆ My **one's place** is **4**.

🚀 **What is my secret space code?** Number: ____________

🎭 "The Great Circus Number Mystery! 🎪"

6) 🎭 A clown wiped off one digit from these numbers! Help the ringmaster restore them!

🎈 _3_7 – The **tens digit** is missing! What could it be?

🎈 1_5 – The **hundreds digit** is missing! Find the missing number.

🎈 _09 – The missing number is **between 5 and 8**. Solve it!

🎈 2_8 – The **tens digit** is **3 more than 4**. What is the missing digit?

🎈 _47 – The missing number is the **sum of 2 and 3**. Find it!

🎈 9_2 – The **tens digit** is the **same as the one's digit**. What is the missing number?

🔢 Place Value Puzzle

7) 🔍 **Clue:** *Rearrange these digits to form the largest number possible.*

a) **4, 7, 2** → Largest number: _______

b) **9, 3, 5** → Largest number: _______

c) **1, 8, 6, 2** → Largest number: _______

d) **5, 0, 9, 3** → Largest number: _______

e) **7, 4, 8, 2, 6** → Largest number: _______

f) **3, 5, 1, 7, 0** → Largest number: _______

🏴☠️ The Treasure Hunt: Find the Hidden Numbers! 🏆

*9) Ahoy, young explorers! The **Lost Treasure of Numeria** is hidden behind secret number codes. Solve them to unlock the treasure!*

🔑 **Clue 1:** The first key is a number with **5 in the tens place** and **3 in the one's place**. Number:

🔑 **Clue 2:** The second key is a number with **2 in the hundreds place, 0 in the tens place, and 7 in the one's place**. Number:

🔑 **Clue 3:** The third key is a number with **8 in the thousands place, 4 in the hundreds place, 1 in the tens place, and 9 in the one's place**. Number:

🔑 **Clue 4:** The fourth key is a number with **6 in the hundreds place, 2 in the tens place, and 5 in the one's place**. Number:

🔑 **Clue 5:** The fifth key is a number with **3 in the thousands place, 9 in the hundreds place, 0 in the tens place, and 8 in the one's place**. Number:

🔑 **Clue 6:** The final key is a number with **7 in the thousands place, 1 in the hundreds place, 4 in the tens place, and 6 in the one's place**. Number:

ADDITION AND SUBTRACTION

Jungle Safari Adventure

Help Ranger Rahul count animals in the jungle!

a) 237 monkeys + 145 monkeys = _______

b) 594 parrots – 219 flew away = _______

c) 144 tigers + 328 leopards = _______

d) 709 zebras – 439 went to another forest = _______

e) 212 elephants + 386 rhinos = _______

f) 691 crocodiles – 278 = _______

g) 192 snakes + 408= _______

h) 821 animals – 395 went to sleep = _______

🏰 Castle Party Nath 👑🍰

Princess Mira needs your help planning a grand feast!

a) 178 guests + 243 guests =

b) 683 guests − 398 guests left =

c) 132 cupcakes + 287 cupcakes =

d) 501 balloons − 267 popped =

e) 365 candles + 147 candles =

f) 200 chairs − 83 were broken =

g) 186 crowns + 226 tiaras =

h) 902 roses − 470 used = _______

i) 399 plates + 165 bowls =

⛺Fun Fair Fiesta! 🎡🎈

You're helping the Fun Fair manager with ticket sales, games, and snacks. Add and subtract carefully!

a) 247 people bought 🍬 cotton candy tickets. Later, 183 more bought them. How many tickets were sold in total?

b) 611 popcorn buckets 🍿 were made, but 259 were eaten. How many buckets are left?

c) 387 balloons 🎈 were inflated in the morning and 225 in the evening. How many total balloons were inflated?

d) 573 prizes 🎁 were on shelves. 318 were won. How many prizes are still there?

e) 402 kids went on the 🎠 merry-go-round, and 134 more joined. How many kids rode the ride?

f) 722 game tokens 🪙 were distributed. 481 were used. How many tokens remain?

g) The clown gave 96 high-fives 🐼. Later, he gave 125 more. How many high-fives in total?

h) There were 623 drinks 🥤 in stock. 321 were sold. How many are left?

i) 488 kids attended the Fun Fair on Friday, and 312 came on Saturday. How many kids in total?

Jungle Adventure

You're tracking animals and supplies deep in the jungle!

a) 153 monkeys were swinging from trees, and 270 were resting. How many monkeys were spotted?

b) 400 bananas were packed for the trip. 165 were eaten. How many bananas remain?

c) 329 parrots flew above, and 147 were seen on branches. How many parrots in total?

d) The camp had 632 bottles of water . Explorers drank 178. How many are left?

e) 233 footprints were seen in the morning and 188 more in the evening. How many total footprints were seen?

f) 503 vines were counted . 197 were cut for the path. How many are still hanging?

g) 306 explorers crossed a rope bridge . 177 more followed. How many crossed altogether?

h) There were 800 jungle hats . 364 got wet in the rain. How many dry hats are left?

🏰 Royal Castle Party 👑 🦢

You're helping prepare the royal ball! Count the decorations, guests, and food.

a) 312 gold plates 🍽 were placed on tables. 164 more were added. How many plates are on the table now?

b) 791 cupcakes 🧁 were baked. 388 were eaten by the guests. How many cupcakes are left?

c) 431 chairs were set in the ballroom 🪑. 139 more were brought in. How many chairs total?

d) 754 candles 🕯 were lit. 276 blew out. How many are still glowing?

e) 145 roses 🌹 were placed in vases. 132 more were added. How many roses in total?

f) 572 napkins were folded. 403 were already used. How many are still unused?

g) 487 musicians 🎻 played during the feast. 128 joined later. How many musicians performed in total?

h) 570 guests arrived in carriages. 245 left after dinner. How many guests stayed?

 Sweet Bakery Bonanza 

Help the baker count cakes, donuts, and orders during a super busy day!

a) 275 cupcakes 🧁 were baked in the morning. 156 were baked later. Total cupcakes?

b) 621 cookies ⊛ were on trays. 349 were sold. How many left?

c) 435 cake boxes 🎂 were packed. 132 more were needed. How many boxes in total?

d) 702 donuts ● were made. 287 were decorated. How many undecorated?

e) 185 orders were placed online. 263 were placed in-store. Total orders?

f) 586 pieces of candy 🍬 were on shelves. 271 were taken. How many remain?

g) 394 lollipops were made 🍭. 127 were broken. How many perfect one's left?

h) 522 pastries 🥐 were ready in the morning. 224 more in the afternoon. Total pastries?

School Day Count-Up

Help the teacher count books, pencils, and students during a school day!

a) 275 pencils were in one box. 168 in another. Total pencils?

b) 813 library books were returned. 412 were borrowed again. How many are left?

c) 301 students attended the morning assembly. 189 came late. How many students in total?

d) 500 chalks were stored. 308 were used. How many are left?

e) 233 papers were printed before class. 186 more during class. Total printed?

f) 754 crayons were shared. 296 were used. How many remain?

g) 491 lunch boxes were counted. 109 more arrived. Total lunch boxes?

h) 668 worksheets were prepared. 253 weren't completed. How many were done?

 Wizard World Wonders ✦ ☽

Join young wizards as they count magic potions, spells, and creatures!

a) 243 magic wands 🪄 were made in the workshop. 161 more were crafted later. How many in total?

b) 721 potion bottles 🧪 were stored. 359 were used. How many remain?

c) 195 fire spells 🔥 were practiced. 198 water spells 💧 too. Total spells practiced?

d) 603 flying brooms 🧹 were parked. 277 flew away. How many still parked?

e) 412 owls 🦉 were in towers. 148 came from the forest. How many owls in all?

f) 584 scrolls 📜 were written. 273 were torn. How many scrolls are good?

g) 347 dragons 🐉 were seen from the tower. 372 flew past again. Total dragons seen?

h) 800 candles lit the Great Hall 🕯. 496 melted. How many still burning?

Nature Trail Tracker

Aarav and Meera went on a long hike.

a) 335 m + 417 m = _______

b) 910 m goal – 742 m walked = _______

c) 235 + 376 + 198 = _______

d) 800 – 380 = _______

e) 139 + 171 = _______

f) 912 – 454 = _______

g) 200 + 418 + 162 = _______

h) 600 – 287 = _______

i) 388 + 119 = _______

✏️ Create Your Own! ✨📚

Use these numbers: **598, 199, 351, 213, 97, 454, 818, 423**

Write your own **addition or subtraction story problem** for each letter.

a) _______________________________
✓ Answer: ______

b) _______________________________
✓ Answer: ______

c) _______________________________
✓ Answer: ______

d) _______________________________
✓ Answer: ______

e) _______________________________
✓ Answer: ______

f) _______________________________
✓ Answer: ______

g) _______________________________
✓ Answer: ______

h) _______________________________
✓ Answer: ______

i) _______________________________
✓ Answer: ______

MULTIPLICATION AND DIVISION

You're spending a busy day in the city! Help solve real-life multiplication and division problems.

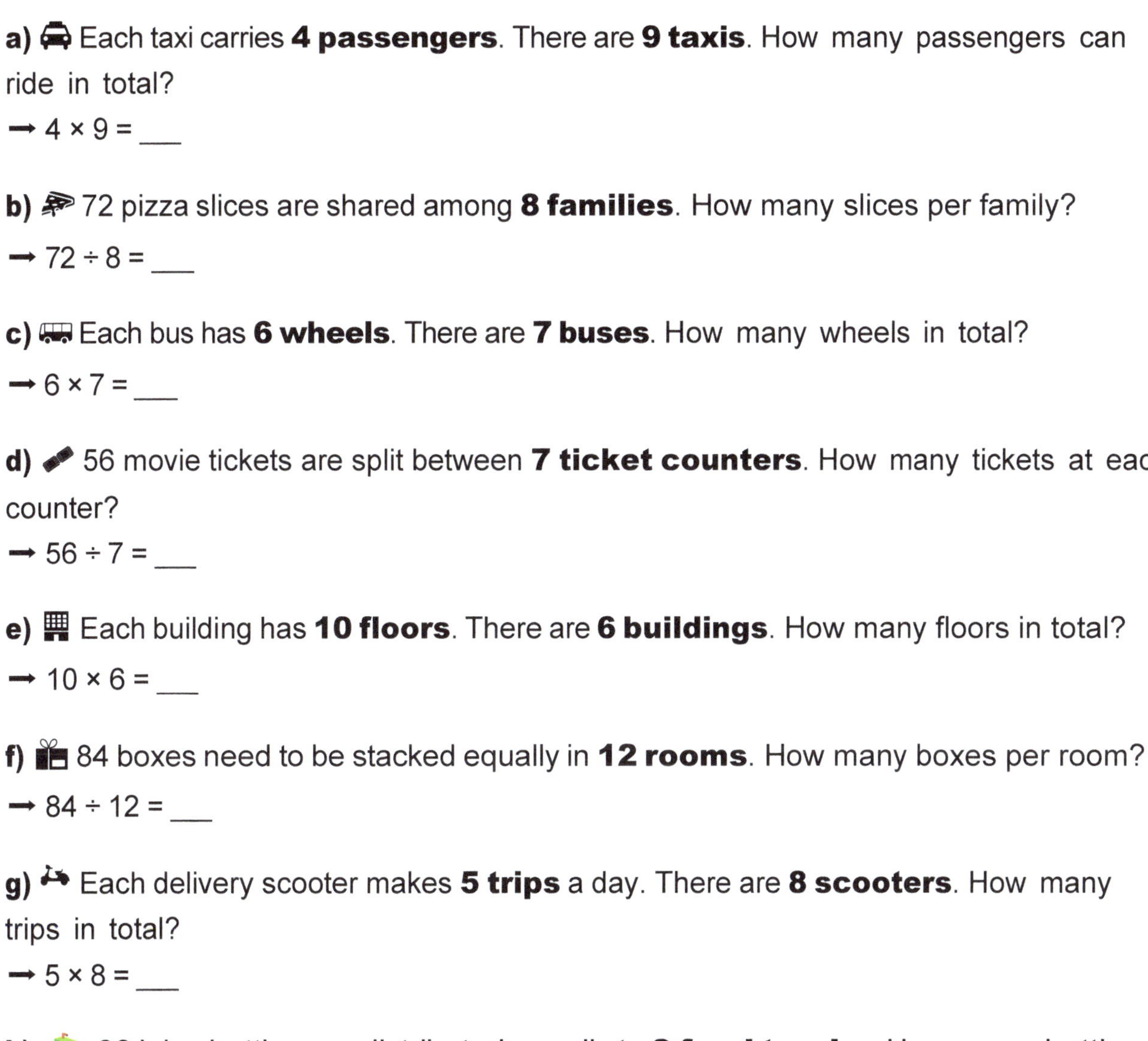

a) Each taxi carries **4 passengers**. There are **9 taxis**. How many passengers can ride in total?

➡ 4 × 9 = ___

b) 72 pizza slices are shared among **8 families**. How many slices per family?

➡ 72 ÷ 8 = ___

c) Each bus has **6 wheels**. There are **7 buses**. How many wheels in total?

➡ 6 × 7 = ___

d) 56 movie tickets are split between **7 ticket counters**. How many tickets at each counter?

➡ 56 ÷ 7 = ___

e) Each building has **10 floors**. There are **6 buildings**. How many floors in total?

➡ 10 × 6 = ___

f) 84 boxes need to be stacked equally in **12 rooms**. How many boxes per room?

➡ 84 ÷ 12 = ___

g) Each delivery scooter makes **5 trips** a day. There are **8 scooters**. How many trips in total?

➡ 5 × 8 = ___

h) 90 juice bottles are distributed equally to **9 food trucks**. How many bottles per truck?

➡ 90 ÷ 9 = ___

Jungle Safari Nath 🐘🌴

You're on a jungle safari! Count animals, trees, and supplies using multiplication & division!

a) 🐒 There are **6 monkeys** on each tree. There are **7 trees**. How many monkeys in total?

→ 6 × 7 = ___

b) 🐘 72 peanuts are shared between **8 elephants**. How many peanuts does each elephant get?

→ 72 ÷ 8 = ___

c) 🐯 Each tiger eats **5 kg of meat**. There are **9 tigers**. How much meat is needed?

→ 5 × 9 = ___

d) 🐦 56 colorful birds are divided among **7 cages**. How many birds per cage?

→ 56 ÷ 7 = ___

e) 🐍 Each snake pit has **4 snakes**, and there are **10 pits**. How many snakes total?

→ 4 × 10 = ___

f) 🍌 You packed **84 bananas** into baskets of **12**. How many baskets?

→ 84 ÷ 12 = ___

g) 🐾 Each jeep can carry **8 tourists**. There are **6 jeeps**. How many tourists in total?

→ 8 × 6 = ___

h) 🐒 You caught **90 photos** of monkeys. You show them equally to **9 friends**. How many photos per friend?

→ 90 ÷ 9 = ___

Sports Day Nath 🏆 🎽

It's school sports day! Use multiplication & division to solve these exciting challenges!

a) Each team has **7 players**, and there are **6 teams**. How many players in all?

➡ 7 × 6 = ___

b) 72 medals are to be given to **8 teams**. How many medals per team?

➡ 72 ÷ 8 = ___

c) Each winner gets 4 **gold stars**. There are **12 winners**. How many stars in total?

➡ 4 × 12 = ___

d) 45 balls are shared among **9 courts**. How many balls per court?

➡ 45 ÷ 9 = ___

e) Each student gets **2 juice boxes**. There are **25 students**. How many juice boxes are needed?

➡ 2 × 25 = ___

f) 96 trophies are divided into **12 boxes**. How many trophies in each box?

➡ 96 ÷ 12 = ___

g) Each relay race has **4 runners**, and there are **11 races**. How many runners total?

➡ 4 × 11 = ___

h) 108 T-shirts were given to **9 teams** equally. How many T-shirts per team?

➡ 108 ÷ 9 = ___

🛍️ Naff Nath Nania! 🛒 🧸 👟

Let's go shopping! Help solve problems at the mall.

a) 👟 Each shoe rack holds 7 **pairs of shoes**. There are **10 racks**. How many pairs total?
➡ 7 × 10 = ___

b) 🍩 72 donuts are shared between **12 boxes**. How many in each box?
➡ 72 ÷ 12 = ___

c) 🧸 Each toy store has **8 shelves**, and each shelf has **5 toys**. How many toys per store?
➡ 8 × 5 = ___

d) 🎁 90 gift items are sorted into **9 baskets**. How many per basket?
➡ 90 ÷ 9 = ___

e) 👜 Each bag counter sells 6 **bags** per hour. There are **7 counters**. How many bags sold in 1 hour?
➡ 6 × 7 = ___

f) 🧃 81 juice bottles are arranged into **9 coolers**. How many in each?
➡ 81 ÷ 9 = ___

g) 🕶 Each sunglasses stand has **3 rows** of **8 glasses**. How many sunglasses in total?
➡ 3 × 8 =

h) 🧼 108 soaps are divided among **9 stores**. How many soaps per store?
➡ 108 ÷ 9 =

FRACTIONS AND DECIMALS

Bake-Off Fractions! 🎂 🥮

You're helping at a bakery! Work with fractions to prepare perfect treats.

a) 🍰 You cut a cake into **8 equal slices**. You ate **3 slices**. What **fraction** of the cake did you eat?

➡ __/ __

b) 🥮 Out of **12 pies**, 3 were chocolate, and 8 were apple. Write the **fraction** of chocolate pies.

➡ __/ __

c) 🍩 You baked **1/4** of a tray of donuts. Your friend baked **2/4**. Who baked more?

➡ __

d) 🍪 If you eat **1/2** of a cookie and your friend eats **1/4**, who ate more?

➡ __

e) 🎂 Add: You decorated **1/6** of a cake, then added **1/3** more. What part is done now?

➡ 1/6+ 1/3 = __

f) 🧁 Subtract: You had **3/4** of a cupcake but ate **1/4**. How much is left?

➡ 3/4 - 1/4 = __

g) 🍫 Out of 10 brownies, you gave 5 to friends. Write the fraction you gave away and **simplify it**.

➡ 5/10 = __

h) 🍪 Are **2/6** and **1/3** equal? Yes or No?

➡ __

🧠 "Fractions & Decimals: Brain Boost Challenge!"

a) 9/3 = _____

b) 5/6 + ⅓ = _____

c) 2/2+13/4 _____

d) ⅞ + 3/2 +8/7 = _____

e) 400/45 =_____

f) 2.5 + 8.35+ 2.5+ 8.35= _____

g) 256.7−98.25 = _____

h) 3.25/4 = _____

i) 125.25/5 = _____

j) Convert 3553 to a decimal = _____

k) Which is greater: 5885 or 0.60.6? → _____

l) Round 87.649 to **1 decimal place** = _____

🧩 Fractions & Decimals: Brain Boost Challenge!

📣 Part A: Fractions Practice

Q1. A chocolate bar has 8 pieces. Ria eats 3. What fraction did she eat?

a) 3/8

b) 5/8

c) 8/8

d) 1/2

Q2. Which is **greater**:
 a)2/3   or b) 3/4

Q3. Are these fractions equal? 1/2 and 2/4 →
Yes / No

Q4. Fill in the blank:
1/4 + ＿ = 1
 a) 1/4

b) 3/4

c) 5/4

d) 4/4

Q5. Circle the largest fraction:

a) 1/9

b) 3/7

c) 2/6

🔢✨ Decimals – Brain Boost Challenge!

Q1. 💡 Match the decimal to its fraction:

0.25 = a) 1/2 👁 b) 1/4 👁 c) 3/4 👁

Q2. 💵 Who has **more** money?

Aman has **$2.80** and Tara has **$2.50**.

a) Aman 🧍 ♂ b) Tara 🧍 ♀ c) Same 💰

Q3. ✔✖ True or False:

0.7 = 7/10 → __________

Q4. 🧠 Fill in the blank:

0.3 + ___ = 1

a) 0.7 🎯

b) 0.5 🎯

c) 0.8 🎯

Q5. 🔢 Arrange from **least to greatest**:

0.6, 0.9, 0.2, 0.75 → ____________________

Q6. What's the place value of **7** in **4.76**?

a) 7 one's 🔢 b) 7 tenths 🔢 c) 7 hundredths 🔢

💭 Fill in the Blanks

a. 0.5 = _____tenths

1. **5**
2. **50**
3. **0.05**

b. 1.00 - 0.25 = _____

1. **0.75**
2. **0.85**
3. **1.25**

c. 0.10 more than 0.60 is _____

1. **0.70**
2. **0.16**
3. **0.06**

🎯 Real-Life Decimals

d. A chocolate bar costs ₹2.75. You give ₹5.00.
☞ How much change should you get?

1. **₹2.25**
2. **₹3.25**
3. **₹2.75**

e. Ravi drank 0.25 L of water in the morning and 0.75 L in the afternoon.
☞ How much did he drink in total?

1. **1 L**
2. **0.50 L**
3. **1.25 L**

f. A pencil is 17.5 cm long. A pen is 20.0 cm long.
☞ How much **longer** is the pen?

1. **2.5 cm**
2. **3.5 cm**
3. **1.5 cm**

↻ Compare the Decimals

g. Which is the **smallest**?

1. **0.6**
2. **0.06**
3. **0.60**

h. Arrange from **smallest to biggest**: 0.8, 0.3, 0.13

1. **0.13, 0.3, 0.8**
2. **0.3, 0.13, 0.8**
3. **0.8, 0.3, 0.13**

i. Which is the **same as** 1.00?

1. **100/100**
2. **10/10**
3. **All of the above**

MEASUREMENT AND TIME

🧠📏⏰ Measurement & Time – Brain Boost Challenge!

📏 A. Lovely Lengths 🚗🪁

1. What is the length of a pencil if it measures 15 cm?
a) 15 mm ▬
b) 15 cm ▬
c) 150 cm ▬

2. 1 meter = _______cm
a) 10 cm ◣
b) 100 cm ◣
c) 1000 cm ◣

3. Which is **longer**?
a) 2 m 🚶‍♀️
b) 150 cm 🚶‍♀️
c) 1 m 🚶‍♀️

⚖️ B. Wild Weights 🐘🍎

4. A watermelon weighs **3 kg**, and a mango weighs **1 kg**. What's the total weight?
a) 4 kg 🍉🥭
b) 2 kg 🍉🥭
c) 5 kg 🍉🥭

5. Which is **heavier**?
a) 500 g 🥐
b) 2 kg 🧻
c) 100 g 🍬

6. 1000 grams = ____kg

a) 1 kg ⚖

b) 10 kg ⚖

c) 100 kg ⚖

🧃 C. Cool Capacity 🍼🚿

7. A jug holds **2 litres** of juice. A bottle holds **1 litre**. How much together?

a) 3 L 🧃 🥤

b) 4 L 🧃 🥤

c) 1 L 🧃 🥤

8. Which container has the **most capacity**?

a) Teaspoon 🥄

b) Mug ☕

c) Bathtub 🛁

9. 1 litre = _______millilitres

a) 100 mL 🧪

b) 1000 mL 🧪

c) 10 mL 🧪

🕐 D. Tick Tock Time ⏳⌚

10. If the clock shows **7:30**, what is the time?

a) Half past 6 ⏰

b) Half past 7 ⏰

c) Quarter to 7 ⏰

11. School starts at **8:00 AM** and ends at **2:00 PM**. How long is the school day?

a) 6 hours 🍎📊

b) 4 hours 🍎📊

c) 8 hours 🍎📊

12. Ravi finished his homework at **6:45 PM**. He started at

6:15 PM. How long did he take?

a) 30 minutes 📋

b) 45 minutes 📋

c) 60 minutes 📋

Think, match, compare & solve! 🎯 🧃

📏 Length Logic 🏃‍♂️📐

a. Who ran the longest?

- Maya ran 950 m 🏃‍♀️
- Anil ran 1.2 km 🏃‍♂️
- Sara ran 980 m 🏃‍♀️

☞ Who ran the longest?

1. Maya
2. Anil
3. Sara

b. Match the objects to their closest length:

- Pencil ✏️
- School bus 🚌
- Door 🚪
1. 6 metres
2. 15 cm
3. 2 metres

c. True or False:
1 kilometre is **shorter** than 800 metres.

1. True
2. False

⚖️ Weight Wonders  

a. A box of flour weighs 2 kg. A bag of sugar weighs 1.5 kg.
☞ What is the total weight?

1. 3.5 kg
2. 2.5 kg
3. 3 kg

b. Which would you measure in **grams**?

1. Your dog 🐶
2. A cupcake 🧁
3. A watermelon 🍉

c. Fill in the blank:
A newborn baby weighs around ______

1. 3 kg
2. 30 g
3. 30 kg

🧃 Capacity Challenge 🚿☕

d. Which holds the **least** liquid?

1. Teacup ☕
2. Bucket 🪣
3. Water bottle 🍼

e. Riya drank 250 mL of juice in the morning and 500 mL at lunch.
☞ How much did she drink in total?

1. 750 mL
2. 850 mL
3. 650 mL

f. Match the items to their approximate capacity:

- Water tank 🛁

- Milk packet
- Medicine spoon

1. 200 mL
2. 1 litre
3. 1000 litres

⏰ Time Tricks 🕐📅

g. What time will it be **2 hours after** 9:30 AM?

1. 11:30 AM
2. 10:30 AM
3. 12:30 PM

h. Your movie starts at 6:45 PM and ends at 8:15 PM.
☞ How long is the movie?

1. 1 hour
2. 90 minutes
3. 2 hours

i. Match each activity to the time it usually takes:

- Brushing teeth 🪥
- A full school day 🍎📚
- Watching a cartoon 📽

1. 2 minutes
2. 7 hours
3. 30 minutes